T0201684

To:...................................

From:...................................

STAR WARS

I LOVE YOU.↓
___

→ I ←

KNOW.
___

Written by Amy Richau

Contents

Introduction

Reach for love and friendship beyond the stars

The relationships you seek are not just in that galaxy far, far away. They can also be close, close at hand. Let this book help you get the best out of all your relationships: whether it's with your friends, colleagues, family, or your soul mate. Duos from Han Solo and Chewbacca to Hera Syndulla and Kanan Jarrus, and sisters Rose and Paige Tico, will inspire you to reach out with your feelings and find ties strong enough to endure the decades, overcome conflicts, and maybe even save a galaxy.

Good-quality relationships make all our galactic struggles worthwhile. Take your lessons from *I Love You. I Know.* and don't let jealousies, separations, miscommunications, or feelings of duty come between your chosen one and you. The wisdom in this book can help you find the right path.

True Love

"I love you."

"I Know."

Leia Organa and Han Solo
THE EMPIRE STRIKES BACK and *RETURN OF THE JEDI*

True Love

Learn how to say, "I love you"

One comes from royalty, the other is a pirate, but Han and Leia don't let their different backgrounds and communication styles get in the way of their romance. Some scruffy-looking nerf herders may show you that they love you before they actually say it out loud! They might show their love by offering you the last bite of their favorite snack, while you're more likely to give your partner lavish compliments or write them a love letter. The key is to stay tuned in to what the other person needs. Remember, what's really important is that you both *feel* loved.

"I feel lost."

Anakin Skywalker
REVENGE OF THE SITH

True Love

Stay in control

Padmé Amidala and Anakin Skywalker's passionate relationship thrived during the Clone Wars, but their love was at odds with Padmé's role as a senator and Anakin's as a Jedi. True love can feel strong and overpowering. But if your feelings are spinning out of control, and you fear their intensity, take a step back and ask yourself why they are having such an effect on you. Are you excited about finding a seemingly rare match, or perhaps you fear being alone? The best way to nurture a love that's positive and long-lasting is to not allow it to have too much of a hold on your life or how you feel about yourself.

"HAD YOU SAID THE WORD, I WOULD HAVE LEFT THE JEDI ORDER."

Obi-Wan Kenobi
STAR WARS: THE CLONE WARS

True Love

Rethink priorities

Endeavor to find balance in the Force (and in your love life). Obi-Wan Kenobi and Duchess Satine Kryze chose to honor the duties of their positions as a Jedi Knight and the pacifist leader of Mandalore, even when that decision meant they could never be together. Your partner and you may find yourselves at a crossroads and forced to make difficult decisions. Whether it's moving farther away or spending more time on a business venture, discuss the dilemma with your partner and express your wishes. And while it's important to think about others, it's your life and your decision. You should be at peace with any choice you make.

"You know how I feel."
"Do I?"

Hera Syndulla and Kanan Jarrus
STAR WARS REBELS

True Love

Communication is key

Some romantic connections are obvious to everyone, but seem to go unspoken between the pair themselves. Kanan Jarrus and Hera Syndulla, space mom and dad to the crew of the *Ghost*, are adept at getting everyone on board the ship organized, but they can't seem to do the same for their own relationship! Your communication style may be the envy of your colleagues, but is it the same at home? Remember to take time out to tell people how you are feeling. You never know what valuable connections you may be missing.

"IT'S BEEN A RIDE, BABE. AND I WOULDN'T TRADE IT FOR ANYTHING."

Val
SOLO: A STAR WARS STORY

True Love

Love without regret

Tobias Beckett and Val's love for each other burned bright as they crossed the galaxy with dreams of their next big score. Beckett and Val didn't play by anyone's rules but their own. The only thing they counted on was their loyalty to each other. If you find the love of your life, dive in and enjoy the ride! Do all you can to preserve and nurture it. While no one can guarantee that love will last, you don't want to look back and wonder what could have been.

Family

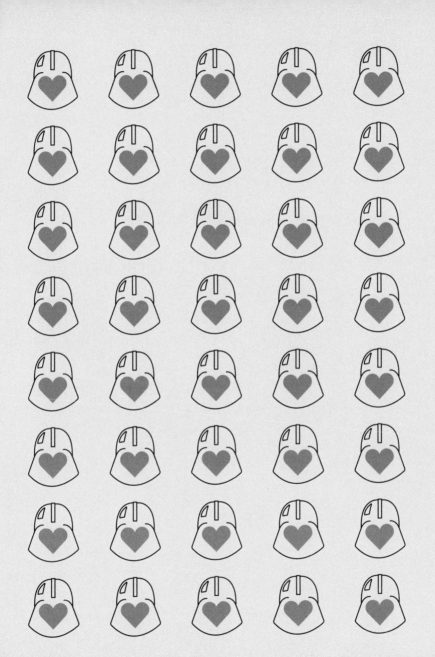

Darth Vader
THE EMPIRE STRIKES BACK

Family

You can't pick your family

Sometimes the villain in the story is a little too close to home. You can't choose who you are related to, but you can choose how much of them you want in your life. Set boundaries and stick to them. Put your feelings and comfort levels first, and make a quick exit if you need things to cool down—especially if lightsabers are involved! If a relative tells you they are ready to change, be open to hearing them out, but remember: actions always speak louder than wheezy, distorted words.

"SOMEHOW, I'VE ALWAYS KNOWN."

Leia Organa
RETURN OF THE JEDI

Family

Trust your bond

Luke and Leia didn't grow up as siblings, but their initial separation didn't hinder the special connection that quickly developed between them. Impactful people can come into your life at any age. The Skywalker twins, each in their own way, helped to rebuild hope across the galaxy while also supporting each other's missions. You might not have a (long-lost) twin, but you might have a friend who feels like one. No matter where your individual journeys may lead you, never stop nurturing your relationship—your bond will only deepen.

"*Whatever I do, I do to protect you.*"

Galen Erso
ROGUE ONE: A STAR WARS STORY

Family

Look for understanding

Separation and estrangement can damage even the most loving relationship, but trust can be rebuilt over time. Galen Erso was forced to choose between keeping his daughter out of the hands of the Empire and leaving his "Stardust" to grow up alone. After years apart, Jyn has to believe her father's expression of love, and trust him to help her take down the Empire. Happy reunions are never guaranteed, but being open to letting wounds from the past heal can bring a new sense of peace and understanding.

"That's how we're gonna win. Not fighting what we hate, saving what we love."

Rose Tico
THE LAST JEDI

Family

Honor loved ones

Sisters Rose and Paige Tico fought with the Resistance against the First Order. When Paige was tragically lost in battle, Rose drew strength from a matching necklace she shared with her sibling. When bad things happen, try not to let feelings of vengefulness and anger overwhelm you. Try to focus on something that would have made your loved one proud, like supporting a charity or cause that was close to their hearts. Carry their memory with you and use it to give you strength as you continue the fight for what you both believed in.

Family

Let go

It's natural to be sad when someone you care for heads off to college or moves to a new city. Loving someone sometimes means letting them go into an unknown world without you. Shmi Skywalker let Qui-Gon Jinn take her son Anakin to an entirely different planet to pursue his Jedi training. As a result, Anakin escaped a life of servitude, suffering, and sand on Tatooine. Consider all the opportunities that will open up for the ones you love and encourage them to do what's right for them. While it's sad to watch them leave, you are helping them find their true path.

Shmi Skywalker
THE PHANTOM MENACE

Friends

"I CAN'T DO THIS ALONE. I NEED YOU IN COMMAND WITH ME."

Poe Dameron
THE RISE OF SKYWALKER

Build a strong network

Whether you're planning a big event for your
friends and family or trying to topple the First
Order, you don't have to do it alone. When they
first met, Poe needed a ship, and Finn needed
a pilot. They gained their freedom and a
friendship when they put their trust and faith in
one another. Together, Poe and Finn grew into
leaders of the Resistance. Look to the people you
trust and admire to give you a helping hand.
Maybe you're better at flying the ship, while your
friend is skilled at shooting down problems.
Build a team with people who complement
your own skills and you'll find that you have
everything you need.

"I HATE YOU."
"I KNOW."

Lando Calrissian and Han Solo
SOLO: A STAR WARS STORY

Friends

Keep competition friendly

There's a reason people encourage "friendly" rivalry. Sharing passions and ambitions with someone can bring you closer together, but it can also make you risk butting heads. Lando Calrissian and Han Solo enjoy many of the same hobbies and vices: smuggling, gambling, and piloting the fastest hunk of junk in the galaxy. Their similarities mean they know never to underestimate (or trust) each other. However, it also means when they come together on a plan, they are a force to be reckoned with. Let competition with your friends help drive you both forward, but don't get lost in a maelstrom of petty squabbles along the way.

"Too many losses.
I can't take it anymore."

"Sure you can.
You taught me how."

General Leia Organa and Vice Admiral Amilyn Holdo
THE LAST JEDI

Friends

Be the spark

Although General Leia Organa and Vice Admiral Amilyn Holdo have a lifelong battle against the Empire and the First Order on their hands, they always maintain their support for one another. True friends look out for each other and inspire one another to do their best. When your friend is facing an uncertain future or they are about to take on a significant challenge at work, stick by their side and be the spark of encouragement they need to keep going.

"NEVER UNDERESTIMATE A DROID."

General Leia Organa
THE RISE OF SKYWALKER

Friends

Know when you have something special

Resistance pilot Poe Dameron knew he had a one-in-a-million-droid in his buddy BB-8. Poe showered the droid with praise after a job well done or any time spent apart. It's easy to overlook coworkers or friends who provide the support you need, day in and day out. If you have someone in your life who is as conscientious and loyal as BB-8, acknowledge their time and effort. Don't let people take them for granted; and when you can, repay the favor of their kindness.

"YOU LOOKED AT ME LIKE NO ONE EVER HAD."

Finn
THE FORCE AWAKENS

Friends

Find true friends

The Force (and BB-8) brought future Jedi Rey and former stormtrooper Finn together, and one of the strongest friendships in the galaxy was born. The unlikely friends saw the good in each other and developed a bond that no amount of separation could break. We all need a person in our lives who just gets us. Seek out real friends— the kind that will always come back for you and love you no matter what baggage you're carrying.

It's Complicated

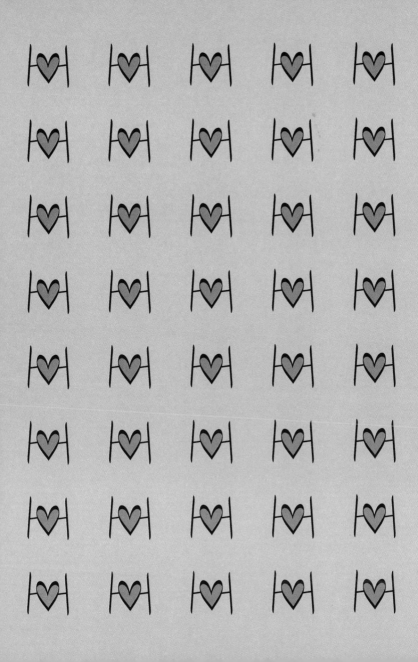

"I HAVE TO SORT THIS OUT ON MY OWN, WITHOUT THE COUNCIL, AND WITHOUT YOU."

Ahsoka Tano
STAR WARS: THE CLONE WARS

Choose your own path

Even when you know it's the right decision, it's hard to part ways from something, or someone, who has been important in your life. When Ahsoka Tano chose to leave the Jedi Order, she broke ties not only with the organization that had betrayed her, but also with her friend and mentor Anakin Skywalker. As challenging as it may be to distance yourself from a friendship, group, or organization, choosing your own path can help you grow as an individual. Your friends and colleagues may miss you, but you never know when your paths will cross again.

"I did want to take your hand. Ben's hand."

Rey
THE RISE OF SKYWALKER

Unexpected connection

When Rey and Ben Solo first meet, they are on very different paths. Rey is a scavenger on Jakku; Ben is a leader in the First Order known as Kylo Ren. Rey tries to convince Ben to join her on her path to the light side, but he is deeply immersed in darker forces. There is balance in everything; accept that people may be stuck in their ways, but do not dismiss their potential for change and redemption. If your connection is positive, you should be able to bring out the good in each other. And with some luck, you could one day find yourself coming together to defeat a common enemy.

"YOU WERE MY BROTHER!"

Obi-Wan Kenobi
REVENGE OF THE SITH

It's Complicated

You can't save everyone

Even when you have the high ground you can't always trust the ones you love to be there with you. Obi-Wan Kenobi trained Anakin Skywalker as a Jedi. Years later, they fought alongside each other as brothers in the Clone Wars. But this wasn't enough to stop the fear and hate building inside Obi-Wan's protégé. You can try your best to instill good in the ones you love, but you can't always prevent them from making poor choices. Lead by example, but know only they have the power to reject the dark side.

"Well, we didn't kill each other, so I guess we're friends now."

Garazeb Orrelios
STAR WARS REBELS

Be open to unlikely alliances

It's easy to write someone off as your enemy when you're on opposite sides of a conflict. Rebel fighter Garazeb Orrelios has every reason to hate Imperial agent Alexsandr Kallus. But after being stranded together on an icy moon, Kallus and Zeb learn they have a lot in common and the seeds of an unlikely friendship grow. People are rarely *all* bad. The person on the other side of a fiery negotiation, or competing aggressively against you for a spot on a team, may be more like you than you realize. Be open to the idea that it's the situation that's the real enemy. Change your mindset and your old adversary could well become your new ally.

"You are the good guy."

Qi'ra
SOLO: A STAR WARS STORY

It's Complicated

Accept that people change

First romances rarely last forever—even if
you believe that person understands you like
no one else. Reuniting with a former love interest
can bring back emotions that feel as strong as
before, but your priorities may have been
changed by time and experience. Don't bet all
your credits on a flight on the *Millennium Falcon*
with your long-lost sweetheart when their mind
is set on impressing their new boss. It will be
hard, but you must accept that the scrumrat
you once fell in love with may not want the
same future you do.

"OH, IT'S BEAUTIFUL."

Director Orson Krennic
ROGUE ONE: A STAR WARS STORY

Avoid destructive relationships

Sometimes love can become misplaced and all-consuming, much like Director Orson Krennic's passion for his beloved battle station, the Death Star. Krennic became obsessed with the weapon, but learned the hard way that a technological terror can't love you back. It's easy to become entranced by things that are shiny and new, but be careful not to lose track of everything else that's important. Whether you are bound up in an idyllic new romance or taken in by an amazing new hobby, it's important to keep perspective.

Enduring Love

"OH MY DEAR FRIEND, HOW I'VE MISSED YOU."

BEEEP DOOP!

C-3PO and R2-D2
THE FORCE AWAKENS

Enduring Love

Forgive quirks

When you've been friends with someone for a long time, they are bound to do things that irritate you—like focusing on the odds of failure when you're about to ask for that raise at work or go on a blind date. Good friends will overlook harmless quirks because they know there are lots of other great things about the relationship. If the moments you spend apart aren't nearly as exciting or fun as when you're together, don't fry your circuit board over the small stuff; treasure the connection you share.

"NOTHING'S IMPOSSIBLE."

General Leia Organa
THE RISE OF SKYWALKER

Long-distance love

While Larma D'Acy commanded Resistance
ground forces, her wife Wrobie Tyce flew
missions across the galaxy in an A-Wing.
Each time they parted, they didn't know when
they'd see each other again, but they each took
their leader General Leia Organa's words to heart
and remained hopeful in the face of adversity.
Every long-term partnership will have its
challenges, and distance can be one of the
hardest to overcome. If you and your partner
have to spend a lot of time away from each other,
focus on why you got together in the first place.
Those positive thoughts should keep your heart
at peace while you wait for a happy reunion.

"CHEWIE, WE'RE HOME."

Han Solo
THE FORCE AWAKENS